ST. JOHN THE BAPTIST CATHOLIC SCHOOL SOUTH BEND, IND.

A Badger Book

MEN OF SCIENCE

by
Dorothy Haas

Illustrated by
J. L. Pellicer

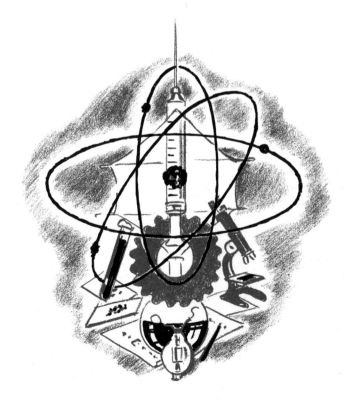

WHITMAN
PUBLISHING
COMPANY
Racine, Wisconsin

CONTENTS

If the people of little Louis Pasteur's village had been asked to guess what he would become when he grew up, few would have said he would become one of the world's greatest scientists. "Little Louis . . ." they would have said thoughtfully. "Well, have you seen any of the pictures he draws? They are really very good. He will probably grow up to be an artist."

Some of the scientist's boyhood drawings still exist. Artists agree that Louis Pasteur, scientist, could have been—Louis Pasteur, artist!

Louis Pasteur

Battle With Death

"Run for your life!"

"Mad wolf!"

A small boy pushed open the heavy door of his home. He slipped inside, slamming it behind him.

His heart pounding, little Louis Pasteur—for that was the boy's name—turned. He brushed aside the lace curtain on the window next to the door. The scene outside was something out of a nightmare.

A maddened, snarling wolf, foaming at the mouth, charged down the street. Panic-stricken people scattered before it. Some found shelter. Others, not so lucky, were bitten. Little Louis closed his eyes. He pressed his face into the scratchy lace of the curtain. But he could not shut out those dreadful cries.

Soon the howls of the suffering beast faded in the distance. Then they stopped altogether. The wolf had gone back to the dark forests that surrounded Arbois. Silence returned to the tiny town.

Once more Louis dared to look outside. A pitiful parade was passing by. One by one, the wolf's victims were being helped up the street. They seemed to be going to the blacksmith's shop.

Louis pulled open the door and followed them. What he saw there was to haunt him for the rest of his life.

The only known treatment for rabies, caused by the bite of a mad animal, was a fearful one. Each of the wolf's victims—eight in all—was brought into the blacksmith's shop. There the doctor touched a red-hot poker to the wounds. He was trying to burn away the poisons left there by the sick wolf.

But the treatment was useless. In the weeks that followed, the wolf's victims sickened. At last, one by one, they died. There was no cure for rabies.

Many years passed. The little boy of Arbois grew up. He studied chemistry and biology. He became a scientist, an honored scientist known throughout France. In his laboratory he found the answers to many grave problems.

The farmers' sheep and cattle died in great numbers from a certain disease called anthrax. Dr. Louis Pasteur found a way to vaccinate them, and so to keep them healthy.

Many people became ill and died from drinking the milk of sick cows. Dr. Pasteur developed a method of making milk safe. We still use that method today. It is called pasteurization.

Many were the problems that the learned Dr. Pasteur solved. But during the years he could not forget the cries of the terrified townsfolk of Arbois.

The trouble was that no one knew quite where to start on the fearful problem of rabies. For nobody knew what caused the disease. Today we know that it is caused by a virus, a germ so small that it cannot be seen under the usual kind of microscope. But Dr. Pasteur did not know this.

One day he was in his laboratory with his assistant. They were talking about rabies, as they often did. The elderly scientist, limping from an illness which had left him painfully crippled, moved up and down the long room as they talked.

"We do not know what causes rabies," he said. He paused for a thoughtful moment, leaning on his cane. "But every problem has an answer," he went on. "And to every answer there is a clue. Let's start looking for a clue. We will begin with the sick animals themselves!"

In the weeks that followed, strange guests came to live in Dr. Pasteur's Paris laboratory: mad rabbits, mad guinea pigs, mad dogs. The scientist studied the disease in these animals. He even studied the saliva which he took from their foaming mouths. But he did not find his clue.

He tried making healthy animals sick in order to test ways of treating them. He injected into them the saliva of sick animals. Sometimes they got sick. Sometimes they did not, or unexpectedly got sick after long months of waiting. Dr. Pasteur was puzzled.

He worked long hours. He was in the laboratory, bent over his microscope, long before his assistant opened the door in the morning. And he stayed on, lost in thought, long after his assistant went home at night.

Months went by. Many times Dr. Pasteur thought he had the answer, only to meet with failure. But he did not give up. And then, at last, the long hours of work had their reward.

He injected nerve tissue from sick animals into healthy ones in a certain way. He found that in doing this he could, without fail, cause rabies in healthy animals. This was because the germs were concentrated in the nerve tissue. And this turned out to be the clue that Dr. Pasteur had been waiting for.

He found that by letting this tissue stand for a few days it became weak. When a dog received this weak nerve tissue

it became sick, yes. But not so sick that it died. The dog got well. And after that, even if injected with the strongest nerve tissue, the dog did not develop rabies. Its body had built up strength against the disease. The dog was "immune."

The scientist knew that persons bitten by rabid dogs do not show signs of illness until nearly a month later. If resistance could be built up in these people before they showed signs of the disease, perhaps they might not sicken at all! He worked up a course of treatment. It would take fourteen days.

On the first day a dose of very weak fourteen-day-old nerve tissue was to be given to a person who had been bitten. This was followed on the second day by a thirteen-day-old dose. And so on, until on the last day strong virus was to be given. During this time the person's body would be building up resistance. Finally, the victim would have so much resistance that he could not get sick.

Dr. Pasteur had found his cure for rabies—or he thought he had. It had been successful with dogs. Would it work as well on a human being? Perhaps it would harm, rather than help, a person who had been bitten!

At last he decided what he would do. He would try the treatment on himself! If he was not harmed by it, then he would be sure that it was safe for everyone.

But something happened before he had a chance to test his cure. It happened on July 6, 1885. Footsteps sounded on the stairway leading to the laboratory. The door was flung open. A woman rushed into the room.

"Dr. Pasteur!" she cried, when she spied the scientist. "I am Madame Meister. I have heard you are working on a cure for rabies. You must help my boy Joseph or he will surely die. We have come all the way from Alsace!"

She turned and pointed to a little boy. He stood in the doorway, smiling shyly at the great scientist. Joseph Meister was nine years old. He had been bitten fourteen times.

Dr. Pasteur stood up, shaking his head. "But, my good woman!" he said. "The treatment has never been tried on a person. It may harm—"

"Please, Doctor!" the woman pleaded. "You are our only hope!"

The scientist was thoughtful. "Let me think," he said. "I will let you know later today."

After Madame Meister and Joseph had gone, the scientist sat down at his desk. Should he use his treatment? Would he be risking great harm to a human life? Perhaps Joseph could live, in spite of his wounds. . . .

He talked to his friends, Dr. Grancher and Dr. Vulpian. These two men knew of his work. They went with him to examine Joseph.

When they had finished, they turned to their friend. "The boy will surely die," they said. "But if you try your treatment he at least stands a chance of living. By all means, try it!"

Treatment began that very day. In the days that followed, Dr. Pasteur and Joseph became good friends. The scientist watched his little friend worriedly. What if the treatment did not help. . . .

At last the day came when Joseph received the last and strongest dose of the nerve tissue. Dr. Pasteur waited. That night the light in his laboratory burned on long after all the other houses on the street grew dark and silent.

Morning came. The sun rose. The city came alive with the sounds of horses and heavy wagons in the street below. Suddenly there was the sound of flying feet on the stairway. Once more the laboratory door burst open and Madame Meister stood there.

"Dr. Pasteur!" she cried. "Come!" She was gone.

Louis Pasteur limped hurriedly after her. At last he reached Joseph's room. He stopped, his hand on the door-knob. What would he find inside? Would his little friend be well, or would he. . . . He pushed open the door.

There, sitting up in the big bed, was a smiling boy. A pale—but healthy—Joseph! Beside him stood his mother, tears in her eyes and a smile on her lips.

Joseph gave a little bound, setting the old wooden bed to creaking. "Good morning, Doctor!" he said to his friend.

The scientist could not answer at once. He closed his eyes and took a deep breath. Thank God! His little friend was alive and well!

At last, once and for all, Louis Pasteur was able to erase from his mind the cries of the people of Arbois.

One dark night in 1864, masked riders swooped down on a small southern farm. When they rode away, they took with them a young slave woman and her tiny baby.

The young woman was never found. But the child, later left to die, was returned to the owner of the farm, Moses Carver.

The Carvers raised the orphaned baby. They taught him all they could. Then, when he was ten years old, they told him he was on his own—to educate himself as best he could.

And that's exactly what young George Washington Carver did! He educated himself so well that he became, at last, one of America's greatest and most honored scientists!

George Washington Carver

Food for the Empty Bowl

"You there, boy!"

A group of boys stood in an Alabama field. They were watching their teacher plow. He was a tall, slightly stooped young man. His dark face was thin and sensitive.

One of the boys turned at the call. He walked over to the fence that separated the field from the road. A man had drawn up there in his wagon. He was watching the boys in the field.

"What's goin' on here?" he wanted to know.

The boy flashed white teeth in a proud grin. "That's our new teacher over there," he said. "Professor George Washington Carver. He's goin' to teach us the right way to plant things here at Tuskegee Institute."

The man threw back his head and laughed. "That's a good one!" he said. "Well, if he's goin' to teach you 'the right way to plant things,' he better find the right kind of

19

plantin' ground first. Why, I been drivin' by this here piece of land every now and then for years. Nobody yet's ever got anything worth growin' off it!"

He clucked to his horse and drove on, chuckling. Just wait until his neighbors heard about this! Those boys, learning "the right way to plant things"—on no-good land!

The boy looked after him for a minute. Then he turned and went back to his classmates. He looked, really looked, at the earth. It was streaked with red and yellow. Great rain-washed gullies crisscrossed it.

The teacher was standing with the boys. He was rolling down his sleeves as he talked. "Now," he was saying, "you saw how I did it. Two of you boys take turns plowing. The rest of you—"

"Mr. Professor?"

The teacher nodded to the boy who had been called to

the roadside. "Yes, Alfred?"

"Professor, that man," Alfred pointed at the wagon moving away down the road, "he says nothin' good ever grew here. If that's so. . . ."

His voice died. How could he ask his question without seeming to say his teacher did not know what he was doing!

Professor Carver finished the question. "How can *we* make something good grow here?" He smiled. "Well, Alfred, it's like this:

"If you've got a bowlful of hominy grits in front of you, and you eat it up, it's gone. There won't be more food in your bowl until your mother puts some there. The bowl is empty.

"Plants are like people—they need food to grow. But this land is like your bowl—empty. There's no plant food left in it.

"The man was wrong about one thing—something good once did grow here. Cotton. And cotton is greedy. It eats up all the food in the land faster than Mother Nature can replace it. But the man was completely right about something else—nothing good will grow here as the land is now.

"So, we're going to help Mother Nature. We're going to fill up this—" he pointed at the land on which they stood, "this 'empty bowl.' Then we'll see what will grow on it.

"Now, you boys divide up into two groups. One group

will go into the swamps. Bring back all the black dirt and leaf mold you can find. The other group will visit farms around the countryside. Ask the farmers if we can have the sweepings from their barns."

As Professor Carver talked, the puzzled frown left Alfred's face. Yes, sir, this new teacher really seemed to know what he was talking about!

When the boys returned with their loads, Dr. Carver showed them how to work the material into the soil. He helped them for a while. Then he went back to his laboratory.

One of the boys leaned on his hoe. "What's the professor *do* in that laboratory of his?" he asked, looking after him.

"I dunno," another boy answered. "But he's a scientist. And everyone knows a scientist's got to have a laboratory!"

A scientist's got to have a laboratory. . . .

George Washington Carver had arrived at Tuskegee from Iowa State College in the fall of 1896. There he had found that his "laboratory" was little more than a room. There was no equipment. There was no money to buy equipment.

But young Professor Carver was used to "making do." He gathered together his students. He told them the kind of things he needed. Then, together, they went out and hunted through the town's trash piles.

Handle-less old pitchers became beakers to hold chemicals. Chipped bottles became flasks. Old dishes, old pots, pieces of string, leather, and wood—all were put to use in unusual ways. Dr. Carver had his laboratory! Without a doubt, there was not another one like it in the whole world!

What wonderful things he did there—things that had to do with the land and the products of the land! If he were explaining it, he might say something like this:

"God and I, we work together in our laboratory. I ask him questions. I work hard. He gives me the answers.

"I ask him, 'Mr. Creator, why won't things grow on this land in the South? Things used to grow here!' Then I go out and bring some of that land into the laboratory. I test it to find out what's in it. I look at it under my microscope. When I begin to think I've got the answer, I say, 'Is that right, Mr. Creator?' And I work some more.

"Pretty soon the answer is right there on my laboratory table for me to see. Southern land has had all the plant food taken out of it! That's why plants won't grow. 'Thank you for helping me, Mr. Creator,' I say. 'That's what I need to

know just now. I'll be back.'
Then I go out and try to teach
people how to put plant food
into the earth."

Professor Carver's ideas
were new to the people of the
South. He had to prove them.

He taught his boys how to
enrich the soil with organic

materials which would decay very quickly. He showed them how to sow crops which would put plant food back into the earth. He taught them how to "rotate" these crops: to plant cowpeas one season, sweet potatoes another, and peanuts a third season. Slowly the boys' poor piece of land improved.

Once the patch of land had shown a loss at the end of a season. Now it began to show a profit. Each harvest, and each profit, was better than the last. Finally, a great day came. The boys planted cotton!

Everybody in the South raised cotton. A good cotton crop brought great profit. The farmers did not know why their cotton crops were, yearly, becoming more poor. They did not understand what was happening to their land.

The boys cultivated their land carefully, as Dr. Carver had taught them. They loosened the soil to discourage the weeds which could harm tender young plants. They waited. They worked. They watched proudly as their cotton grew tall and strong. And at last it was time to harvest.

Professor Carver stood out in the field. He looked at the boys working, picking the cotton. The cotton! He looked at it—great, fluffy puffs of white fiber spilling

out of the bolls. It was a bumper crop; the boys had a right to be pleased. Suddenly he heard a noise behind him. He turned. A man had drawn up on the road next to the field.

The man was staring at the cotton. His eyes were round with wonder. He shook his head. "Well, I swan!" he said. "How did those boys get cotton like that to grow on this worn-out old land!"

His hands clasped behind his back, Dr. Carver walked over to the fence. "This land used to be 'worn-out,'" he said, smiling. "But it isn't any more. We built it up."

"But who—how—" The man was speechless. Build up land? He had never heard of such a thing.

A boy approached them. "Professor Carver," he said, "you're wanted over at your laboratory."

"Say!" the man exclaimed. "You must be that professor fellow I saw here with these boys a few years back! Do you mean to say you know how to do things like this? You sure ain't no ordinary farmer!"

Dr. Carver's eyes sparkled. "I'm a scientist," he said, "a specialist in agriculture and botany. And," he went on, with a smile, "a scientist who is wanted at his laboratory!" He turned and started away.

"Say, there—Mr. Professor," the man called.

Dr. Carver turned. "Yes?" he asked.

"Uh—well, you see," the man said, "I got a patch of land that's hardly fit for pasture any more. Maybe you could tell me how. . . ."

Dr. Carver nodded. "Next time you pass here, bring along a sample of your land. I'll be happy to analyze it for you and tell you how it can best be developed."

"I sure will, Professor," the man said, clucking to his horse. "I sure will!" Just wait till he got home and told his neighbors about *this*!

Dr. Carver looked after him. Here was one man who was ready to accept his teachings. There would be others. And one day the soil of the South would be rich again.

He turned and moved away toward his laboratory. Work was waiting for him there.

Young Henry Ford had a dream: a small car that everyone could afford to own. Luckily, his dream didn't end with the invention of the car itself. He went on to invent ways of producing his car.

Standard parts for cars? Assembly-line production? Henry Ford put these new ideas to use. His car-building ways were adopted by the entire automobile industry.

Henry Ford

Dreamer on Wheels

The inside of the little brick shed was lighted by a flickering kerosene lamp. In its dim light a man worked over a machine—part bicycle, part carriage, part engine. The man's face was pale and tired. Great, dark shadows showed under his eyes.

"Henry Ford!"

The voice came from the doorway. The man looked up. His wife stood there. Her nightdress and slippers showed underneath the fringed shawl she had wrapped around her. Rain dotted the big black umbrella she carried.

"Henry," she said, "it's two o'clock in the morning! You simply must get some rest tonight, or you'll—"

"Clara," her husband said mildly, "you'll catch cold, out here in the night air." He grinned at her. "But I'm glad you came, anyway. Look, here!"

As his wife moved closer, he reached into the engine.

"We fasten this," he said, "to—this. And—we tighten—this nut—a bit more, and"—he picked up an old rag and wiped his hands—"we are ready to try this horseless carriage, this 'quadricycle'!"

Clara Ford forgot the lateness of the hour. "Do you mean to say it's ready to test right now—this minute?" she said, her eyes round.

Henry grinned at her. "Right now," he said. "There couldn't be a better time. There won't be any horses on the street to be scared by the noise. And anyway, I just can't wait until tomorrow!"

He pushed the automobile—for an automobile it was—out of the shed. He started the engine.

"If this thing works right tonight, I'll give you the second ride in it tomorrow. That is," he called back over his shoulder, "if you have a cup of good hot chocolate ready for me when I get back."

Clara waved after him. "It will work right," she called. "I'll have the second ride in it. Your chocolate will be waiting, Henry."

Henry turned out of the alley. He drove down Bagley to Grand River Avenue. From there he turned onto Washington Boulevard.

He had to be careful. The streets were dark. The paving bricks did not always fit tightly together—where there were paving bricks! Some of the streets were unpaved. The ruts were slippery in the rain.

He took a deep breath of the misty, warm air and smiled to himself. His gasoline-engine-driven carriage worked just fine.

It was a bit noisy, of course. He looked up at the silent, dark houses. The noise didn't seem bad enough to wake anyone, though. Detroiters certainly were sound sleepers!

Satisfied, he turned his little automobile and headed back toward Number 58 Bagley Avenue, toward his cup of hot chocolate and a few hours of much-needed sleep.

The months that followed were busy ones. During the day he worked at his job as engineer at the Edison Illuminating Company. At night he worked in the little shed on Bagley Avenue.

The horseless carriage, the "quadricycle," became an everyday sight around Detroit. At the sound of its sputtering, chugging engine on the street, people ran out of houses and stores. They lined up on the sidewalks to watch it pass.

Drivers of carriages had to hold a tight rein on their horses. The animals were terrified by this noisy, smelly beast that raced past them at speeds up to twenty miles an hour.

The men with whom he worked knew of Henry's experiments. Some of them thought he was wasting his time.

"Where could you ever get

enough gasoline to drive the thing?" they said. "Now, with a horse—why, you just turn it out in the nearest pasture!"

Other men thought he had an interesting invention. Few of them went so far, though, as to say it had a future. "Who ever could build enough of them to go around," they said, "even if people did want to buy them!"

In August of that same year, 1896, four men from the Edison Company were chosen to go to New York. A big meeting was being held there for Edison men from many parts of the country. Henry was one of the men chosen to go to the meeting.

The meeting went on for several days. On the last day a dinner was held. Present at the dinner was the master inventor himself—Thomas Edison, the Wizard of Menlo Park!

During the meal, talk turned to cars that were then being built. Some cars ran on the principle of the steam engine. Their fires had to be fed. Water in boilers created steam, which made the cars run.

Other cars were run by electric batteries. These were silent and smooth running. But, since batteries go dead, they could not travel far from electrical charging stations.

"Mr. Edison," said one of the men from Detroit, "this young man"—he pointed at Henry—"has built a gasoline-engine-driven carriage. He drives it around Detroit, scaring all our horses half to death!"

Thomas Edison turned and looked at Henry. "You don't say!" he said. Here was a young man who worked for his company, an electric power company—and yet who built a gasoline-powered carriage!

Henry felt his face grow red. Would Mr. Edison be angry?

Thomas Edison wasn't angry. He smiled. "Here, young fellow," he said. "Sit next to me. I want to hear about this invention of yours."

Henry moved into the seat next to Mr. Edison. He swallowed. But then he forgot to be nervous as he began to talk on his favorite subject.

"You know how a gasoline engine works, sir," he said. "Mine has two cylinders. Power goes from the engine to the wheels by a system of belts and chains."

He went on to explain the workings of his invention. "The car carries its own fuel," he said. "A tank under the seat holds three gallons of gasoline. Altogether, it's a light motor, meant to drive a light carriage. It *has* to be light," he added with a smile, "to run on our rutted dirt roads!"

Talk at the table had stopped. Everybody was listening to the young fellow from Detroit. Most interested of all was Thomas Edison.

Henry finished. "That's about it, sir," he said. "If you ever come out to Detroit, I'll be happy to give you a ride in it."

Thomas Edison dropped his fist to the table so hard that the china rattled. "That's it!" he exclaimed. "That's the kind of mechanical carriage we need!

"It doesn't need an engineer and a fireman to run it, like the steam-driven carriage. It doesn't need to stay near a power station, like the electric carriage. Young man," he said, "you're working on the kind of thing that may some-day replace the horse and carriage. Just keep at it!"

Henry left the meeting and took his train back to Detroit. He didn't join in the talk of the three other men. He looked out of the window and listened to the sound of the wheels on the track. "Just-keep-at-it! Just-keep-at-it! Just-keep-at-it!" they seemed to be saying.

And keep at it he did. He kept at it until the Ford automobile became one of the most familiar pieces of machinery on the North American continent!

35

Many inventors have been badly handicapped by lack of money. If anything, Guglielmo Marconi's problem was just the opposite!

He was the son of a wealthy man. It would have been easy for him to live a life of leisure. Instead, he chose a life of worthwhile work—and in doing so, enriched the world with his inventions.

Guglielmo Marconi

Wizard of Wireless

Nobody in the port city of St. John, Newfoundland, happened to look up at Signal Hill on a certain windy December day in 1901. If they had, they would have been surprised. "Now who can be up there flying a kite on a cold, gray day like this!" they would have said.

For a kite there was, whipped about by a brisk wind. It rose several hundred feet above the plateau on top of the hill. But it was no ordinary kite. It was much larger than a man. Fastened to it was a thin wire. The wire was an antenna. It ran down a pole and into a barracks.

Inside the building were three men. They were grouped around a strange instrument, a receiving set. The antenna was fastened to it.

One of the men, younger than the others, bent over it. He held an earphone to his ear with one hand. With the other he slowly turned a knob on the receiver. There was

a frown on his thin, alert face.

"Do you hear anything, Marconi?" asked Kemp, the engineer.

Guglielmo Marconi shook his head. He went on listening for the three clicks which were the Morse code signal for the letter S. The men at Poldhu, England, were to have started sending the signal nearly three quarters of an hour before. That would be eleven thirty, Newfoundland time. It was now past noon, and still they had not picked up the signal.

Paget, the other engineer, spoke. "Perhaps some trouble at Poldhu . . . ."

"No," Marconi said. "I do not believe they were held up. The signals are there. We must simply find the right wave length in order to receive them."

As he worked over the receiving set, Marconi thought back to the days when he had first become interested in sending messages through the air. Only seven short years before, he had still been living with his mother and father on their estate near Bologna, Italy.

"Mama . . . Papa . . ." the young Guglielmo said, as a maid carried away the dinner plates. "Will you come upstairs with me to my workshop now? I have something to show you."

"Now what kind of trick are you working on, up in that room of yours, Guglielmo?" asked his father. "I sometimes think you should be a magician!"

Alfonso, Guglielmo's older brother, defended him. "This is no magician's trick, Papa. You will see."

The Marconi family rose from the table. They followed young Guglielmo up to his workroom. They talked as they climbed the stairs.

"I have been reading," Guglielmo told them, "about work done by a German named Heinrich Hertz. He is able to send electric waves across

a room from a special oscillator that he constructed. He can cause a spark to appear on a receiver many feet away."

"So. You wish to make sparks in the house, eh, Guglielmo?" his father said. "Maybe you should set this receiver thing in the fireplace. We do not wish to have our house burned down!"

The family laughed. At the top of the curving stairway they turned into a small room. They grouped around a strange little box that was set upon the table.

"No," Guglielmo said, "I am not going to send a spark across the room. The house will not burn down. Listen!"

He touched a button. In the distance a bell rang.

"Eh? Somebody downstairs rings a bell?" his father said.

Alfonso laughed. "Not somebody downstairs, Papa. Somebody here! Guglielmo rang the bell!"

"But how?" said their father. "I see no wires!"

"Don't you understand, Papa?" Guglielmo said. "There are no wires! The bell rang because of the electrical waves I sent out here. They were picked up downstairs and caused the bell to ring." He touched the button again and the bell tinkled in the distance.

The elder Marconi shook his head. "A nice parlor trick," he said dryly. "It should be of great use to bell ringers!"

The young inventor was patient. "It's a beginning, Papa. I am going to try to make the charges stronger. That will increase the distance they travel. Perhaps some day we will be able to send signals great distances without connecting wires—from city to city and country to country."

"Perhaps," his father replied. "But I cannot help thinking it is an unlikely thing you try to do!" He turned and made his way out of the room.

Guglielmo's mother paused beside her son. "Do not be downhearted because of your father's words," she whispered. "I am sure that when the time comes he will be willing to help you, as he always has." She patted her son's shoulder and followed her husband.

Guglielmo continued to experiment. Alfonso continued to help whenever possible.

Guglielmo worked over his sender, strengthening it. Soon the signals it sent out went greater and greater distances.

He moved out into the garden and sent signals the length of it. He found that by raising his sending and receiving equipment into the air, he strengthened the signals even more.

Signor Marconi came into the garden one day. He watched his son tapping out Morse code signals on a sender set up beyond the terrace. Alfonso, hundreds of feet away at the other end of the garden, waved his handkerchief when he received the signals. *Signor* Marconi paced off the distance. It was such that Alfonso could not possibly have heard the sounds without a receiver.

He went back to his youngest son. "Guglielmo," he said, "you need money for your work. I will put a certain sum of money in the bank for you to use." He turned and walked away.

Guglielmo grinned after him. "Papa," he called, "if you will go down to the receiver with Alfonso, I will send you my thanks in Morse code—by wireless!"

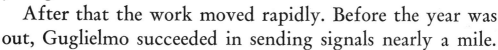

The older man turned. He smiled and waved at this eager young son of his.

After that the work moved rapidly. Before the year was out, Guglielmo succeeded in sending signals nearly a mile.

He went to see people in the Italian Government. He told them about his invention. But they were not interested. "Of what *practical* use can this be!" they exclaimed.

The young inventor then went to England. There he patented his equipment. He made more tests. He sent messages from Poldhu in Cornwall to Crookhaven, Ireland, more than two hundred miles away.

He proved, too, that his invention was useful. He set up sending and receiving equipment on an English lightship, the *East Goodwin,* and at the South Foreland lighthouse.

One stormy night the lightship was struck by another ship. Signals went out. The South Foreland received the signals. Lifeboats were sent to the ship. The men on the *East Goodwin* were saved.

Marconi continued his tests, always improving his equipment. He developed better aerials. At last he was ready for the real test. He, Guglielmo Marconi, was ready to try sending his signals across the Atlantic Ocean!

"I am sure it can be done," he said. "All that is needed is sending equipment strong enough to hurl our electromagnetic signals into the air, and receiving equipment powerful enough to reach up and bring them back to earth. And I believe we now have such equipment!"

Was that a faint click he had heard just then? Marconi's fingers paused on the dial. He listened closely. No, nothing. His imagination at work! Slowly he moved the knob. The sound was there, waiting to be picked up. He had to find it.

Many people said messages could not be sent so great a distance. Signals could not, they said, cut through wind, rain, snow, or fog. Or they said the signals would go straight out into space and could not be brought back to earth. Much depended on this test today.

There it was again! That faint sound, a tiny click. Marconi stiffened. He listened, pressing the earphone against his ear. Then, as the kite, whipped by the wind, carried the antenna high into the air, the sound came through, sharp

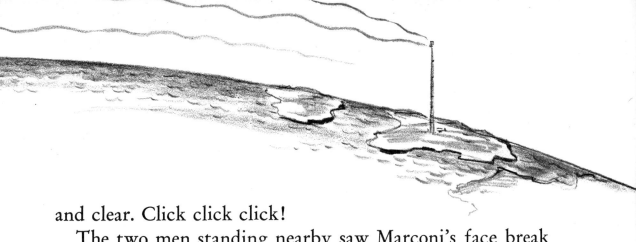

and clear. Click click click!

The two men standing nearby saw Marconi's face break into a smile. He looked up at them.

"Listen," he said, handing the earphone to Kemp. "Do you hear it?"

The engineer listened. "There's no doubt about it!" he exclaimed. "That's the letter S in Morse code—three sharp clicks. It's what we've been waiting for! Here, Paget," he said to the other engineer, "see what you hear."

Paget smiled as he listened. "We've got it all right!" he said. "Congratulations, Marconi!"

Marconi stood up. "Just think!" he said. "Those signals came to us from nearly two thousand miles away! Why," he said, "who can say, perhaps one day we will even be able to hear the human voice itself—by wireless!"

"Which of the Wright brothers," people sometimes ask, "was more responsible for inventing the airplane?"

The brothers would have laughed at such a question. For the answer is: one was as responsible as the other! They thought as a team; when one had an idea, the other was sure to improve on it. And they worked as a team; when they flew their gliders and, finally, their plane, each took a turn at the controls while the other acted as assistant.

The airplane is the amazing result of true teamwork.

Wilbur and Orville Wright

Men With Wings

"Katharine?"

A pretty, dark-haired woman hurried into the front hall of a big old home in Dayton, Ohio. She looked up the stairway. Her father, Bishop Milton Wright, was leaning out of his study door.

"Was there any mail from the boys?" he asked.

Katharine Wright shook her head. "Not a word," she said. "Certainly they must have tested their plane by now! And—" she sighed, "oh, Father, I hope they'll be home for Christmas! Why—why, it's only a week away! And Christmas just wouldn't be *Christmas* without Wilbur and Orville here at home . . . ."

"Careful—watch that wing!"

"Some wind! Must be blowin' up to twenty-five miles an hour! Fasten those ropes!"

Seven men crowded around a machine, a flying machine, on a lonely strip of beach at Kitty Hawk, North Carolina. They were trying to keep the machine from being carried away by a wind that whipped the sand into clouds around them.

Five of the men wore seamen's clothing. They were from the Life Saving Station on Kill Devil Hill at Kitty Hawk. The other two men wore business suits and high starched collars.

"Set it down on the track," said Wilbur Wright. "But

hang on until we get the guide ropes tightened."

"Too bad you have to make your tests today in this wind," said one of the seamen.

"Tomorrow might be just as windy," answered Orville Wright. "And besides, we couldn't wait many more days and still hope to be home for Christmas."

They fastened the ropes to the airplane and stood back. The wind quieted for a minute. In the silence could be heard the dull roar of the mighty Atlantic. The lonely cries of sea gulls echoed overhead.

"My stomach says it's nearly noon," said one of the seamen.

Wilbur took out his big silver watch. "So it is," he said, looking at it. "Well, let's try just once more before we stop to have something to eat."

"It's your turn to fly the machine, Will," said Orville. "Remember to use a light hand on that rudder."

It was December 17, 1903. Wilbur and Orville Wright had already made three very short flights that morning. They had flown as far as 175 feet, and had been air-borne about twenty seconds on the longest of these flights.

These had been unsteady, up-and-down flights. The plane would rise to fourteen feet from the ground, and then it would dart, suddenly, to within ten feet. The brothers hoped to make a longer flight. They wanted to prove beyond doubt that this was a real, motor-driven flight, and not just a wind-lifted glide.

Many men in the past had thought of flying. Some had even tried. They had been able to fly gliders for very short

distances. But nobody had been able to put a motor-powered plane in the air and keep it there.

Wilbur and Orville Wright believed this could be done. They did not listen to people who laughed and said, "If men had been meant to fly, they would have been given wings."

As boys they flew kites. They tried to understand what kept the kites in the air. And they watched the birds. "See how the birds use their wings," they said. "They certainly know things about the air that we don't know!"

When they grew up they built a glider. They flew that. They made many hundreds of glider flights. Then they decided to build an airplane that would stay in the air longer than a glider could.

Their ideas were different from those anybody else had. And so they built a small wind tunnel and tested these new ideas. And at last, in their little bicycle shop in Dayton, they built their plane.

It was made of light wood, wire, and canvas. Even using these light materials, they figured it would weigh nearly 750 pounds with a man in it.

It was powered by a four-cylinder gasoline engine which could deliver twelve horsepower. Instead of wheels, the plane had runners like a sled. These runners rested on a track about sixty feet long. The plane moved along this track until it picked up enough speed to take off.

After they had their plane built, they decided to take it to Kitty Hawk to test it. "The winds there are usually steady at this time of year," they said. "And besides—the sand is soft, if we should have an accident!"

After months of hard work, they were going to find out if their ideas were good. They were going to find out if their plane would really fly.

A brisk gust of wind caught at Wilbur's cap. He reached up and turned his cap around so that it wouldn't blow off his head. Then he turned up his coat collar and climbed into the plane. He lay down on his stomach and grasped the steering wires.

"Start the motor, Orv," he called back over his shoulder.

Orville worked over the little motor for a minute. It coughed. Then it caught hold. The plane shuddered.

"All right, men," Orville called. As the rope holding the plane slipped away, it moved slowly down the track. Then it picked up speed. Orville ran beside it, steadying the wings.

He didn't need to run the full length of the track. As the plane picked up speed it rose into the air.

"Good luck, Will," Orville shouted over the roar of the motor. He stopped running and watched the plane lift uncertainly into the air. Once again it flew unsteadily for a short distance. Then, caught by the wind, it dipped dangerously near the earth.

"Ahh-hh-hh . . . ." chorused the men who watched.

"Lift that left wing, Will!" Orville shouted, unmindful that his brother could not hear him.

Then, as suddenly as it had dipped, the plane righted itself. Orville held his breath. Would it be able to . . . ? It would—and did! The plane leveled off and flew an even, steady, controlled course!

"Just look at it go!" shouted one of the men.

"He's really flyin'!" cried another.

Orville let out his breath. He stood looking after the plane. Flight! Motor-powered flight! For the first time in history, man was actually flying!

Suddenly one of the plane's wings tilted. A fresh gust of wind caught it. The plane pitched toward the earth. It came to rest on a small, sandy dune. The motor died. The screams of the sea gulls were loud in the stillness.

The men ran forward. Their feet slipped in the shifting sand. As they drew near they saw Wilbur scrambling out of the plane.

"Will! Will!" Orville called. "Are you all right?"

Will grinned at them as they puffed across the dune and crowded around him. "I'm just fine," he said. "And, Orv, we did it! I just checked the watch. I was up fifty-nine seconds, and"—he looked back at the starting track—"covered something more than eight hundred feet!"

The seamen pumped the brothers' hands. "Congratulations!" they shouted.

"Most amazing thing I ever saw!" said one of them in wonder. He glanced up at the sea gulls soaring overhead. "Not quite as spry as them gulls up there," he laughed. "But I wouldn't doubt," he said, looking from one brother to the other, "that soon you men will be outflyin' them birds!"

Bishop Wright looked up from the slip of yellow paper which had just been delivered to him. He was smiling. "It's from Orville," he said. "They flew their airplane. It says here that they made four flights in it!"

Katharine clasped her hands. "Oh, Father," she said. "How very happy they must be! I'm proud of them!"

"And," Bishop Wright went on, "you'll be pleased about this, my dear, he says they'll be—"

Katharine's eyes sparkled. She didn't give her father time to finish the sentence. She flew to the dining-room door. "Carrie!" she called. "Will you order an extra-big turkey, please? Mr. Orville and Mr. Wilbur will be"—she turned and flashed a smile at her father—"*home for Christmas!*"

When you turn on your television set, or listen to your radio, or enjoy a sound movie, or place a long-distance telephone call, do you ever wonder about what has made these things possible? Probably not! They are so much a part of our modern world that we take them for granted.

None of them would have been possible, though, were it not for a small electronic tube called the "Audion Tube." Without it we would not have such present-day wonders as electric eyes, electronic brains, electron microscopes, cyclotrons, rockets, and satellites. Lee de Forest, the inventor of the Audion Tube which made all these things possible, might well be called the Father of the Electronic Age!

Lee De Forest

The Mystery Tube

In a poor little hall bedroom on Chicago's Washington Boulevard, a young man sat at the key of a small wireless set. He touched the key. Then he stopped to tinker with the set.

It was early on a September evening in 1900. The young man's name was Lee de Forest. He was working on an invention, one he called a "Responder." It would increase the speed with which wireless signals could be received.

The young man was absorbed in his work, hardly aware of his surroundings. Suddenly he looked up. He glanced around the room. What had caught his attention?

Everything seemed in order. He turned back to his set and went on with his tinkering. Then, his eyes wide, he spun around and looked across the room at the gas light on the far wall. Something had changed just then!

His eyes fixed on the light, he touched the key—dash

dot dot dot. Across the room the gas light dimmed and glowed in the same rhythm—dash dot dot dot. It dimmed when he sparked the coil, brightened when he cut it.

Excitedly he sparked the coil again and again. Each time the result was the same.

Was it possible—astonishing thought—that electromagnetic waves put out by his little sending set could be received by a gas flame? It was an amazing idea. He forgot about work on the Responder. The rest of that evening he experimented with the astonishing new thing. He wrote down the results of his experiments. Then, regretfully, he put away his notebook until he would have time to work along this exciting new line.

The years between 1900 and 1903 were busy ones for the young inventor. He moved to New York. There he set up The American de Forest Wireless Telegraph Company. He finished his Responder. And he found a fine assistant, a young fellow named Clifford Babcock.

At last, one day in 1903, he got out his old notebook. He began to work on the idea that a heated gas unit could, in some way, be put to use in the field of wireless.

He already knew that his first idea had been wrong. The gas flame had not been affected by electromagnetic waves. It had been affected by *sound* waves.

Cliff Babcock came into the laboratory ready to work. He glanced across the room, startled by what he saw.

Lee was hunched over a strange setup: a small battery, and a Bunsen burner with two electrodes fastened within the flame. A wire, fastened to one of the electrodes, ran to

a water pipe where it was grounded. A second wire, fastened to the other electrode, ran out the window and up to an aerial. The whole thing was attached to a telephone receiver which Lee held to his ear.

Cliff crossed over to stand next to him. He stood frowning, puzzled by the queer-looking equipment.

After a minute Lee looked up. He handed the receiver to him. "Hear anything?" he asked.

Cliff listened. After a minute his eyes grew round. "Why," he exclaimed, "you're actually picking up Morse signals! But how?"

Lee turned off the gas in the burner. "I don't quite know the 'how' of it—yet," he said. "But I mean to find out."

He went on to explain his idea about heated gases. "I'm sure," he finished, "that this idea can be used in some way for wireless reception."

Cliff was thoughtful for a minute. Then he grinned. "Well, when do we begin?" he asked.

"Now!" laughed Lee, slapping him on the back.

As one, they bent over the equipment. Lee turned the

key on the burner and touched a lighted match to the gas. As it flared, he said, "I should imagine I'll have to find another way to heat the gases. Flame isn't practical. It's too dangerous for common use. And there'll have to be some kind of container for the electrodes and the gas. Now I think we can somehow heat the gas electrically and. . . ."

And so began months of work. The months stretched into years. The eager young inventor tested many ways of heating his gas. And he tested many containers for the gas and electrodes.

Finally he hit upon using an ordinary light bulb, which has a single filament and from which the air has been pumped. Just two changes—but what important changes! —were necessary. His tube would have two filaments, one of carbon and the other of platinum, and it would contain a certain amount of gas.

He took his plans to a manufacturer of light bulbs. In a few days he hurried into the laboratory. He had the tube.

He put it in place in the wireless set. Then he picked up the receiver and listened for a minute.

"It works, all right," he said quietly, handing the receiver to Cliff. Then he sat back and looked thoughtfully at the tiny tube. Something bothered him. It worked, and yet he wasn't satisfied.

Suddenly he pushed back his chair and went to a corner of the lab. He dug around in a drawer and hurried back to the wireless set. He held a piece of tin foil.

"Here, Cliff," he said, "let me at that tube for a minute. I've got an idea."

He took the tube from the set and wrapped the strip of foil around it. He explained as he worked.

"If I wrap this tin foil around the tube, and attach it to the antenna, we'll have a third electrode on it."

"A *third?*" asked Cliff. "But what for?"

Lee shook his head. "I don't know, exactly," he said. "But it seems to me we'd have more strength in the signals if we did. It's possible that with a third electrode, the tube will be even more effective."

He set the foil-wrapped tube in place, lifted the receiver —and listened to signals louder than any he had ever heard! The third electrode—that did it! It made his tube more sensitive than any being used in the field of wireless! He handed the receiver to Cliff.

Cliff listened. He shook his head in wonder. "Lee," he said at last, "you've done it! This is *big!*"

Lee held down his excitement. "It may be, Cliff," he said. "But we can't be sure until I have the third electrode put inside the tube. I'll see about it early tomorrow morning."

As he talked he had been removing the tube from the set. Now he held it up.

"You know, Cliff," he said, "we can't go on calling this thing the 'thing'! And we certainly can't call it the 'three-electrode vacuum tube'—that would scare people half to death!"

Cliff nodded. "I know," he said. "I've been thinking about that too. How about calling it the Audion Tube? That's from the Latin verb *audire,* 'to hear.' And it's easy to say. . . ."

Lee was quiet for a minute. "The Audion Tube," he said slowly. "Say, that's good, Cliff! The Audion Tube it is!"

A few evenings later Lee and Cliff went into the wireless station next to the lab. Lee carried a small, wooden, sealed box. The new Audion Tube could be seen through the glass in the cover of the box. He set it down carefully on the table next to the sending set.

"Clear with one of the ships out in the harbor, will you, Burch?" he asked the operator. "Ask them to send *D*'s for ten minutes "

Burchard, the operator, contacted the ship. Then he looked on curiously as the men hooked up the wooden box.

Lee put on the headphones. He adjusted the tuner knob

and listened. The sounds of the code came through, loud and clear. Dash dot dot!

Dash dot dot! A pleased smile spread over his face. Without a word he handed the earphones to Cliff.

Cliff slipped them on and listened. He looked up and grinned triumphantly. Then he quietly passed the earphones to Burchard.

The operator listened. Then he jumped up, his eyes wide.

"Will you listen to those signals!" he exclaimed. "I've been an operator for a long time, but I've never heard signals as strong as those! What's *in* that box, anyway?"

Lee and Cliff chuckled at his astonishment. They unhooked the box.

"I can't tell you just yet, Burch," Lee said regretfully. "But rest assured you'll be hearing a lot about it soon!"

Back in the lab, Lee set down the precious box. He dropped into his swivel chair, stretching out his long legs in front of him.

"Well, Cliff," he said after a minute, "there it is—the work of more than two years!"

He was quiet for a minute, looking at the little box.

"Well, small as it is," he went on, "I've got a feeling about it—a feeling that our little box may well hold the most gigantic thing in the entire field of sound. Why, who knows, it may even hold such secrets as we haven't dreamed of—" he flashed a grin at his assistant "—yet!"

Penicillin was discovered quite by accident. And it was more than ten years before practical ways of producing it were found. Nevertheless, Alexander Fleming knew the worth of his discovery. Years later he showed the original mold culture to reporters; he had preserved it!

He was knighted in 1944. In 1945, along with Dr. Ernest B. Chain and Sir Howard W. Florey who found ways of producing penicillin, he was awarded the Nobel Prize.

Sir Alexander Fleming

Yellow Magic

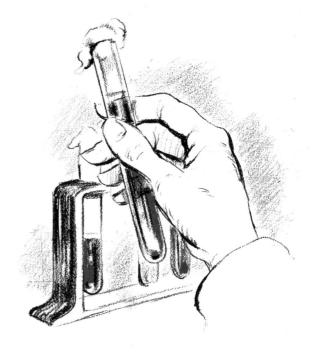

In a quiet little laboratory in St. Mary's Hospital on London's Praed Street, a scientist bent over his microscope. He was studying something in a little glass plate called a Petri dish. He looked intently into his microscope for a long moment.

At last he wrote something in his notebook. Then he put aside the Petri dish. He reached for the glass cover to place over it. But before he could cover it, something happened to the dish.

A tiny speck, too small to see, floated in the air above the laboratory bench. The movements of the scientist's arm sent up faint air currents. They caught the speck and wafted it down into the Petri dish. It settled there just before the cover glass was slipped into place. It was a tiny spore, the seed from which mold grows.

Since the mold spore was nearly invisible, the scientist

did not see it settle in the dish. If he had, he might have thrown away the contents of the dish at once. For the dish held a special kind of bacteria being grown on a special, pure bacteria food. It was called a "culture." Anything falling into the culture ruined it for laboratory work.

But the scientist didn't see the mold spore fall into his dish. And so the culture was kept.

The scientist was Dr. Alexander Fleming. He was a bacteriologist. His business was the study of those tiny organisms which are the terror of mankind—bacteria which cause sickness and death.

At the moment Dr. Fleming was working on a paper about a certain kind of bacteria. In order to see them, he had grown the bacteria in his laboratory. He studied them carefully as he worked on his paper. The year was 1929.

Several days passed after the mold spore dropped onto the culture. Once again Dr. Fleming reached for the Petri dish. He took off the cover and placed the dish under his microscope. Then he looked into the instrument's eyepiece. He straightened in surprise.

"Why, what's this?" he said aloud.

He glanced at the window. Praed Street was hidden by a thick London fog.

"Frightfully damp weather!" he exclaimed. "Good for mold, though. Well, as long as it's there, let's have a closer look at it!"

He leaned over his microscope once more, frowning thoughtfully.

The single mold spore had sent out many tiny arms. These had, in turn, sent out arms of their own. The spot of mold had grown bigger and bigger. What Dr. Fleming saw in his microscope was a regular little colony of soft, furry mold growing on top of the bacteria culture.

Suddenly he blinked.

What was that? He adjusted the eyepiece of his microscope and looked more closely. The tiny spot of mold had a ring around it. The ring was free of bacteria. Now here was something interesting!

Dr. Fleming took a test tube. He filled it with a kind of broth, the kind mold likes to grow on. Then, using a platinum wire loop, he picked up some of the mold on the culture. He was very careful not to take any of the bacteria with it. He set the mold down on the broth in the test tube. Then he sealed it with cotton and held it up to the light.

"There, now, little fellows," he said. "Let's see what

you'll do in a culture that's all your own!"

He set the mold culture aside to grow. Then he went back to his work on the bacteria culture. His paper had to be done on time.

Several more days went by. The paper was finished and sent off. At last the scientist was free to look at his guests, the mold which had dropped in without invitation and had been asked to stay. He found that the test tube now had a fine growth of fuzzy mold on top of the broth.

Dr. Fleming dipped up some of the mold. He streaked it across a glass plate. Then he put certain bacteria on the plate. He set it aside and waited to see what would happen.

After a few days he looked at the plate. Some kinds of the bacteria had grown right up to the mold. But other kinds could grow nowhere near it; they had been stopped by it. And they happened to be kinds of bacteria which had always meant serious illness, even death, to man!

Now here was something a bacteriologist could get excited about!

Dr. Fleming knew that certain kinds of bacteria have pitched battles. Each side sends out strong chemicals to try to poison the other side. The stronger bacteria win the war by killing the weaker bacteria.

But nobody had ever suspected that mold could declare war on bacteria—and what's more, win that war!

Dr. Fleming set a great many test tubes of mold culture to growing. Then he dipped up some of the mold and smeared it on a glass slide. He took it to another scientist who knew all about plant life.

"Can you tell me what this queer-looking mold is?" he asked. "It dropped into one of my cultures."

The other man put the slide under his microscope.

"Oh, it's a common-enough mold," he said after a time. "Likes to grow where it's cool and damp. Our London housewives are doubtless having their troubles with it this summer too. In weather like this it spoils enough bread and cheese to feed the king's guard for a week!"

He gave the slide back to Dr. Fleming. "It's one of the penicillium family," he said. "I'm not exactly sure which branch of the family it belongs to, though."

Dr. Fleming went back to his laboratory with the slide. Common mold, eh? Well, for a common mold, this little colony of mold spores was performing some very *uncommon* tricks!

Months passed. Dr. Fleming soon had racks of test tubes,

each with a velvety pad of mold on top. He performed many experiments.

As he worked with the mold, he became acquainted with its habits. He found that it did something unusual; it turned the broth on which it grew a brilliant, golden yellow. This gave him a new idea. Maybe the fluid produced by the mold could also kill bacteria!

He began a new series of tests. He streaked his plates with the yellow fluid. He put bacteria on the plates. And he had his answer: the yellow fluid did kill the bacteria!

All of Dr. Fleming's tests had been made on the bacteria themselves. Now he tested the fluid on living cells. The cells did not seem to be harmed by the golden fluid. Was it possible that a fluid so powerful that it stopped bacteria growth would prove harmless to living beings? Dr. Fleming made a last series of tests.

He took his golden fluid and went to the room where laboratory animals were kept. He injected it into well animals and into sick ones. Then he waited.

Days passed. Each day he visited his little animals. The healthy ones showed no signs of becoming ill. And sick animals, which ordinarily would have died, improved quickly and soon were well. It almost seemed a miracle!

The last day of the animal tests found Dr. Fleming standing before the cages. He was watching the rabbits nibble at their lettuce. The young medical student in charge of the animals stood next to the scientist.

"The stuff you gave them certainly seems to agree with the little chaps!" he said. "Why, that little fellow over

there was dying last week! What did you give him, sir?"

Dr. Fleming found a crisp piece of lettuce. He held it inside the cage for the rabbit to nibble.

"It's a filtered fluid produced by a mold of the penicillium family," he explained. "Since I can't very well call it 'mold fluid' "—he smiled—"I call it 'penicillin.' "

The young man tried the word. "Penicillin—penicillin. A queer word, but I imagine one could get used to it."

Then another idea came to him. "I say, Doctor!" he said. "How did you happen to find out that pen—penicillin could cure sickness?"

Dr. Fleming was quiet for a minute, remembering. "It started as something of an accident," he said finally. "After that it was a question of patience and work—good, satisfying work!"

The young man remained next to the rabbit cages after the scientist left the room. He looked down at the rabbit and shook his head.

"Well," he exclaimed, "all I've got to say is: It's a lucky day for the human race when 'accidents' happen to men like Dr. Fleming!"

In 1905 an unknown young man wrote a very special paper and published it in a scientific magazine. The young man's name was Albert Einstein. The paper was about something he called the "theory of relativity."

At the time it was published, few men realized how important this
paper was. That was because almost nobody understood it! Gradually,
though, learned men came to understand that Albert Einstein had discovered one of the laws of nature!

Albert Einstein

The Letter That Changed History

"So you see, my daddy said I should be careful about taking up your time. He said your time is very valuable and I've probably been bothering you."

The unhappy little boy stared down at his sneakers. Then he looked up at the old man who sat beside him in the dappled shade of a big oak tree. The child squirmed uncomfortably.

"If I've been bothering you, I'm sorry!" he blurted out.

The old man to whom he spoke would have been known almost anywhere in the world. People everywhere agreed that his was one of the greatest minds of his time. His name was Albert Einstein.

He was listening carefully to this troubled child—as carefully as he would have listened to any of the great men who so often sought him out. He listened carefully, even though his own mind was troubled by a grave problem. He

73

put aside his own worry, for a time, to talk to his little friend.

The boy was quiet. Professor Einstein puffed thoughtfully at his pipe. His dark eyes, serene when he was thinking, were apt to twinkle unexpectedly when he smiled. Now, even though he didn't smile, they twinkled slightly as he said, "You are afraid you waste your old friend's 'valuable' time, eh, Jimmy?"

The boy looked up and nodded vigorously.

Professor Einstein leaned down and tapped out his pipe into the gravel of the garden path.

"Jimmy," he said, "*every* man's time is valuable. When he is doing something he really wants to do—talking to a friend, for instance—why, an hour seems like a few minutes. And that is time well spent."

The little boy's face brightened. "Then you don't mind when I come to see you?"

Professor Einstein shook his head. "No, Jimmy. You needn't worry about 'bothering' me."

The boy gave a gusty sigh of relief. "I'm glad!" he said simply.

"Professor! Professor Einstein!" Two men were hurrying up the path. They carried brief cases.

Seeing them, Jimmy jumped up. "Good-by, sir," he said hurriedly. "Be seeing you," he called, ducking through an opening in the hedge.

The scientist rose and went to meet his callers. They were Dr. Leo Szilard and Dr. Eugene Wigner, two well-known physicists. At sight of them, Professor Einstein could feel the full weight of a world problem settle on his shoulders once again.

His little friend Jimmy's trouble was the kind that could be easily taken care of. But his own problem was something else again. It was one that nobody could help him solve. He, and he alone, had to decide whether he should sign his name to a paper which would start work on a most terrible weapon of war.

Dr. Szilard and Dr. Wigner had come to see Professor Einstein a month ago. They had brought him papers written by Dr. Szilard and Dr. Enrico Fermi. The papers told about experiments carried out by these two men. The experiments were based on Einstein's mass-energy theory, part of the theory of relativity, of thirty-five years before.

The papers said that it was possible that something could be done which man had once thought impossible. Certain kinds of atoms, it now appeared, could be split to release tremendous amounts of energy. This process—the scientists called it "nuclear fission"—could be used in the making of giant bombs.

The scientists had reason to suspect that work on the atom was moving forward with great strides in Germany. The Government of the United States had to be warned of this. Work on nuclear fission had to be started at once.

Albert Einstein was the most famous scientist in the United States. His name, signed to a letter, would add weight to information which must be put before the Government.

"It's good to see you again, gentlemen," Einstein said, shaking the men's hands. "Come. Let's go inside where we can talk."

He led the way indoors. The men followed him. They settled themselves in the comfortable chairs in his study.

One of the men opened his brief case. He took a type-written sheet of paper from it and held it out. Professor Einstein took it without looking at it.

"I have thought a great deal about this, since you left me last month," he said softly. "I have read the manuscripts in

question and. . . ." He sighed. There was sadness in his great, dark eyes. "I agree. Nuclear fission is now a definite possibility."

He turned and looked out the window at his garden.

The two men across from him watched him. They glanced at each other. It was a heartbreaking decision this fine old man had to make.

His back to the two men, Einstein read the paper he held in his hand. It was a letter addressed to Franklin D. Roosevelt, President of the United States, at the White House in Washington, D.C.

It told the President of the work done by Dr. Szilard and Dr. Fermi, and of their belief that uranium could be made to release energy different from any that man had ever known. It said that if a bomb, based on this principle, were exploded in a port, the entire port and some of the land around it would be destroyed. It told the President that Germany might already have some of this information. It said all the things the three men had talked about a few weeks before.

Einstein finished reading the letter. He turned, letter in hand, and went to his desk. He hunted through the stacks of books and papers until he found a pen.

With the pen held above the letter, he looked up at his two visitors. The sadness was gone from his eyes. Determination was written there instead.

"It is true that nuclear fission may be used destructively," he said. "But—and it is of this that we must think—it may also be used as a great force for good!

"If we can accomplish it, nuclear fission accompanied by a self-sustaining release of energy may well be the most important event of the twentieth century. Who knows but that it might even change the entire course of history!"

He leaned down and signed the letter, "Very truly yours, Albert Einstein."

Thus it was that, on August 2, 1939, the way was opened for the beginning of the Atomic Age!

On a gray December day in 1942, a strange telephone call was made between Chicago and Cambridge, Massachusetts. Dr. Arthur Compton, director of the Manhattan Project, was calling Dr. James B. Conant, chairman of the National Defense Research Committee. Because the United States was at war, they spoke in a kind of code. Nobody listening in could have understood them. But Dr. Conant knew of secret experiments being carried on in Chicago. He understood.

"I have just left the Italian navigator," said Dr. Compton. "He has arrived safely on the shores of the new world."

There was a tension-packed pause at the other end of the wire. "Oh?" said Dr. Conant after a minute. "And how did he find the natives?"

"Friendly!" said Dr. Compton happily. "Most friendly!"

Enrico Fermi

The Italian Navigator

A scholarly-looking man hurried down Ellis Avenue on Chicago's south side. An icy wind whipped winter's first snowflakes about him. But he stepped out briskly, breathing deeply of the cold air. Dr. Enrico Fermi—physicist, university professor, Nobel Prize winner—enjoyed the outdoors.

He turned in at a big stone entrance built like an old castle. It was the west gate of Stagg Field, the University of Chicago's unused football stadium. Inside, he made his way to a building that sat huddled beneath the deserted west stands.

Once the building had been a squash court. It had echoed with the *squash!* sound of a little black ball and the excited calls of the boys who played there. But the building was a squash court no longer. Now it was called the "Metallurgical Laboratory." The scientists who worked there were sworn to absolute secrecy. Their mysterious experiments had

nothing at all to do with the science of metals! The squash-court laboratory had become a top secret division of a United States Government agency called the "Manhattan Project."

The scientist paused in the hallway of the building. He slipped out of his overcoat and shrugged into a lab coat that was streaked with black. Then he turned toward the lab. A young man was just coming out. He too wore a grimy lab coat. And he had been handling something black, as the smudges on his cheek gave proof. Whatever the experiments going on in the little building, one thing was certain—they were dirty!

Seeing his chief, the young man stopped. "Morning, Doctor," he said. He nodded down at a bottle he carried. "They're mixing the cadmium solution over at the lab right now. It'll be ready when you need it."

"And the check list?" asked Dr. Fermi.

"That's ready too," the young man said. "It's with your things up in the gallery."

He moved on. Dr. Fermi went on into his laboratory—into a forbidding, dusky scene.

The walls of the room were black. The floor was black. At one end of the room, surrounded by a boxlike wooden

framework, was a big black ball, flattened on top. The ball was made of graphite, the material commonly found in lead pencils. It was dust from the graphite ball which had turned everything in the laboratory an eerie black.

But never mind the dust! That graphite ball—the scientists called it a "pile"—was going to do something that few men believed possible. It was going to split the atom!

Atoms might be called the building blocks of all matter. The chairs we sit in, the food we eat, the water we drink, the air we breathe, the clothes we wear—all are made up of atoms. But atoms cannot be seen. They are almost the tiniest particles imaginable.

Imagine that you have an iron ball, one which can be cut in half as easily as an apple. Then suppose you cut one of these two pieces in half. Imagine that you keep on dividing the ball in this way, always taking one piece and cutting it in half. At last nothing would remain but a single, tiny invisible speck of iron—an atom. Imagine that you can see this atom.

You would find it made up of several parts, all of them constantly moving. The parts are called protons, neutrons, and electrons. The protons and neutrons form the core, the nucleus, of the atom. The electrons spin around the nucleus at amazing speed. The parts of the atom are held together by an enormous strength. Try as you might, you couldn't cut the last atom of the iron ball in half.

Scientists had known of atoms and this hidden strength for many years. They had often talked about how wonderful it would be if the tremendous energy holding the atom together could be set free for man's use. But they had always thought that it would take more energy to split the atom than could be obtained from the division. Then, late in the nineteen thirties, certain discoveries were made, discoveries which shed light on the inner workings of the atom.

One man in particular thought the atom could be split to obtain unheard-of amounts of energy. And what's more, he thought he knew how to do it! He was Dr. Enrico Fermi, an Italian physicist. Dr. Fermi had come to live in the United States when he found that he was no longer able to live under a fascist form of government.

Dr. Fermi had done much work on the neutron. This work had won the Nobel Prize for him. It was work which led directly to the building of the first atomic pile at the University of Chicago.

Neutrons, said Dr. Fermi, could be made to shoot into the cores of atoms, splitting them apart. Furthermore, he said that once the process was started, the neutrons set free would act upon other atoms, releasing still more energy and even more neutrons. He called this process "self-sustaining chain reaction."

The scientists faced many problems in trying to split the atom. But one problem stood out above all the others. Neutrons moved with lightning speed. A way had to be found to slow them down in their headlong flight. Otherwise they would fly off and be lost before they did their atom-splitting work.

The scientists tested many materials which they hoped

might slow down the neutrons. At last Dr. Fermi thought he had the answer.

"Pure graphite should slow down the neutrons," he said. "Let us make a pile of graphite and uranium. When we have built it to just the right size, more neutrons will be trapped within the pile than can escape from it. When that happens, neutrons will begin splitting the uranium atoms and will continue to do so in a chain reaction."

Materials were hard to find. Ordinary graphite was plentiful enough. But absolutely pure graphite had to be made. And that took time. Further, uranium was very scarce.

Materials arrived slowly at the laboratory. But arrive they did. At last, in the spring of 1942, the scientists were able to begin. They piled up the graphite and uranium around a source of free neutrons which would set off the pile. Then they tested it with sensitive instruments.

Yes, Dr. Fermi decided, they seemed to be on the right track. But their pile had to be bigger; too many neutrons were still escaping from it. They took down the small pile. In the fall of 1942 they began another, a bigger, one.

The materials were placed in layers. First a layer of graphite bricks was put down. This was followed by a layer

of bricks which had pieces of uranium sealed in their hollowed-out cores. Slowly the pile took shape.

At last the day came when the pile was ready to be tested. It was December 2, 1942.

Dr. Fermi walked around the pile, looking at it. The big black ball nearly touched the ceiling. He slid his hand along one of the control rods.

"In these slim rods," he thought, "lies the safety of all the people in this laboratory!"

The control rods were made of cadmium. They were thrust deep into the center of the pile. There they soaked up neutrons in much the same way sponges soak up water. When they were pulled out of the pile, the neutrons would be free to split the uranium atoms. If anything went wrong, if the pile began reacting too fast, the control rods would fall back into place. They would stop the action of the pile.

Further, a group of three young men would be seated on a platform above the pile with jugs of cadmium solution. If

danger threatened, they would break the jugs. The solution would pour down into the pile. It would help the control rods soak up neutrons. The young men were jokingly called the "suicide squad."

But nothing should go wrong! Figures are truthful. Mathematics had told the scientists just how to build the pile. Mathematics had told them what would happen inside of it.

And yet. . . . The scientists were like men who know all about flying from having studied about it in books, but who have never actually flown a plane. As atom-splitters, the scientists knew all about it from their figures, but they had never actually split an atom. The control rods were like automatic pilots, ready to take over in case of trouble.

Fermi turned to a young scientist working nearby. "Is everything ready here on the floor?" he asked.

"Ready as it'll ever be," the young man answered. "All of the rods except one will come out before we begin. I'll handle the last one myself. You just give the orders."

Satisfied that everything was running smoothly on the main floor, Dr. Fermi went up to his place in the gallery.

His instruments were placed there. They would tell him, minute by minute, what was going on inside the pile. With these instruments, he would chart a safe, steady course for the reaction which would take place inside the big pile.

The morning hours slipped away. The instruments were checked and rechecked. Everyone in the laboratory had a job. Everyone went about his work quietly and surely.

At last Dr. Fermi looked at his watch. The test could begin. The floor around the pile was cleared. Only the young scientist in charge remained—and the suicide squad perched above the pile.

All the scientists who had worked on the project crowded up into the gallery. There was excited chattering.

"Keep your eye on the counters!"

" . . . what this will mean if. . . ."

" . . . what people in the neighborhood would think if they. . . ."

Gradually a hush settled over the group. All eyes turned to Dr. Fermi. He did not show excitement. He was calm.

"We will withdraw the last cadmium rod inches at a

time," he said. "Each time we will check our instruments.

"Ready down there?" he called to the main floor.

"Ready," came the cool reply.

"Now!" commanded Dr. Fermi.

The watchers grew tense. The young scientist pulled the rod a little way out of the pile.

At once the instruments in the gallery showed what was happening inside the pile. The steady click click click of the counters began to sound faster. Lights flashed on the panels. The first few neutrons were shooting into uranium atoms!

Dr. Fermi watched his instruments carefully. He noted the changes they showed. He was like a ship's captain moving through dangerous, shallow waters. A ship's captain takes soundings, tests, before he moves ahead. Dr. Fermi was taking his own kind of soundings; only when the nervous clicking of the counters leveled off into a steady rhythm, showing that the way ahead was safe, did he give the order to move forward.

"All right," he called. "Pull out more of the rod."

Once again the watchers tensed. And once again they relaxed. Nothing more than a quickening of the instruments showed what was happening below.

Morning wore into afternoon. Little by little the long rod was pulled from the center of the pile. Little by little activity inside the pile increased, then leveled off. A full reaction could not take place as long as any part of the rod remained in the pile.

At last, at 3:25, the final order was given.

"The rest of the rod can now come out of the pile," said Dr. Fermi.

There was no sound in the laboratory—not from the men who watched, nor from the big pile itself. But the instruments told their story. The lights flashed the message for all to see. The counters clicked excitedly for all to hear.

Inside the big black ball neutrons which had no means of escape were slamming into uranium atoms. They were splitting those atoms, releasing a new kind of energy, greater than any man had ever known.

Dr. Fermi was silent. He studied his instruments for a long time.

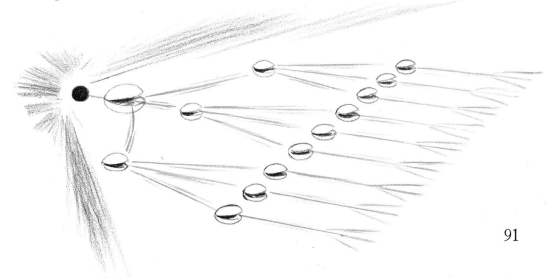

"You can replace the rod now," he called then, and turned to the scientists who had helped to build the pile.

"The pile created a half watt of power," he said. "The amount is really quite unimportant, as you must realize, since we can increase it at will."

He looked around him, smiling quietly. "What is really important," he said, "is that we have established something new here today—a self-sustaining chain reaction!"

Hubbub broke out in the gallery. Amid the congratulations and the slapping of backs, Enrico Fermi's mind was far away. "Science has opened the doors to a wonderful new world today," he thought. "Who knows what great wealth awaits us there!"